ON THE
CORAL REEFS

BY SNEED B. COLLARD III

Marshall Cavendish
Benchmark
New York

To Lexa,
For sharing your passion for our underwater planet.
—Sneed

ACKNOWLEDGMENTS

With special thanks to Dr. Alexandra Grutter, School of Integrative Biology, University of Queensland, Brisbane, Australia, for countless hours explaining the amazing world of cleaner fish; also for her helpful reading of the manuscript. Additional thanks to her colleague Redouan Bshary for discussing his work; to Dr. Grutter's husband, Mark Johnson, for providing many of the spectacular underwater images in this book; to Michael Arvedlund, for sharing his clownfish enthusiasm and interesting research; and finally, to Anne Hoggett and Lyle Vail of the Lizard Island Research Station for making it possible for me to experience Australia's Great Barrier Reef for myself.

Marshall Cavendish Benchmark
99 White Plains Road
Tarrytown, New York 10591-9001
www.marshallcavendish.us

Library of Congress Cataloging-in-Publication Data
Collard, Sneed B.
On the coral reefs / by Sneed B. Collard III.
p. cm. — (Science adventures)
Summary: "Describes the work of Dr. Alexandra Grutter and other biologists in the field of coral reef relationships"—Provided by publisher.
Includes bibliographical references and index.
ISBN 0-7614-1953-5
ISBN-13 978-0-7614-1953-2
1. Coral reef ecology—Juvenile literature. 2. Coral reefs and islands—Juvenile literature. I. Title. II. Series.
QH541.5.C7C65 2005
577.7'89—dc22   2004030316

Series design by Anne Scatto / PIXEL PRESS

Photo research by Linda Sykes Picture Research, Inc., Hilton Head, S. C.
Stephen Frink/Corbis: front cover, 2, 5, 12, 26; Royalty-free/Corbis: back cover; Jeffrey Rotman/Corbis: iii, 6, 24, 29, 31; Mark Johnson: iv, 8, 16, 18, 22; Fliip Nicklin/Minden Pictures: 4; Birgitte Wilms/Minden Pictures: 7; Lawson Wood/Corbis: 10; B. Jones/ M. Shimlock/Photo Researchers, Inc.: 11; Bill Varie/Corbis: 14; Natalie Fobes/Corbis: 20; D. Parer and E. Parer-Cook/ Auscape/Minden Pictures: 27; Theo Allofs/Corbis: 30; Fred Bavendam/Minden Pictures: 32; NOAA/NCDC: 35; Corbis: 37.

Printed in Malaysia
35642

FRONT COVER: Coral reefs provide homes for a wealth of different species. Their beauty and wonder also attract millions of snorkelers and divers each year.
BACK COVER: Butterflyfish are just some of the spectacular species that depend on coral reefs to survive.
TITLE PAGE: Corals look beautiful, but they are effective predators. Here, a cup coral captures and stings a very small octopus.

Contents

Introduction

Humans are only beginning to understand the richness and complexity of life on Earth. Every day, scientists are making new, startling discoveries about the wonderful planet we call home. This series seeks to share the lives and adventures of a few of these scientists as they probe the mysteries of places as diverse as coral reefs, rain forests, and the deep sea.

On the Coral Reefs explores the relationships that make coral reefs some of Earth's most fascinating ecosystems. There's no better way to introduce these relationships than with the scientific research of Dr. Alexandra Grutter. Dr. Grutter has spent the past decade investigating tiny fish called "cleaner fish." These fish set up cleaning stations where other fish come to have their parasites removed. Dr. Grutter's discoveries about cleaner fish have changed how scientists think about coral reef relationships. But cleaner fish and their "clients" are only one important relationship found on the reef. As you turn the following pages, you will encounter the worlds of clownfish, giant clams, and the corals themselves. Each depends on other organisms to survive, and their relationships make our planet a richer place to be.

OPPOSITE: Dr. Alexandra Grutter is one of many marine biologists who study the fascinating world of reef relationships.

Diving In

R. ALEXANDRA GRUTTER signals to her dive buddy and flips backward over the edge of her fourteen-foot boat. She waits for her partner to join her in the water. Then they both deflate their air-filled life vests and sink beneath the surface of the Coral Sea.

Kicking smoothly with her long white fins, Alexandra—or Lexa, as her friends know her—heads almost straight down. After thousands of dives, she swims like a fish and feels almost as comfortable underwater as she does on land. Visibility isn't great today, but that doesn't bother her. When she's about thirty feet down, she spies large coral outcrops beginning to take shape in the bluish gloom. Lexa's breathing rate increases along with her excitement.

Swimming slowly, Lexa and her dive buddy follow the line of under-water outcrops. They glide over living corals shaped like tables, brains, mushrooms, and fans. Schools of damselfish, butterflyfish, sweetlips,

OPPOSITE: Dazzling scenes such as this one greet divers at every turn on coral reefs.

A school of fish whizzes by a coral reef. While some coral reef fishes live in large groups like these, many others prefer a more solitary existence.

and other fish swirl past the divers and dart between the endless cracks and crevices in the corals.

Suddenly, something special catches Lexa's eye. It is a large grouper wedged between two corals. The enormous fish stretches five feet long and weighs at least a couple of hundred pounds. But Lexa isn't interested in the grouper. She's interested in a tiny pair of striped fish darting in and out of the grouper's mouth and gills. The tiny fish are called *cleaner wrasses,* or cleaner fish, and Lexa has dedicated most of her career to understanding their remarkable lives.

Crazy about Coral Reefs

Dr. Grutter is just one of thousands of scientists who devote their lives to studying coral reefs and their inhabitants. It's easy to understand why.

Like living jewels, coral reefs sparkle beneath many of the earth's tropical waters, from Africa, Asia, and Australia to Central America and the Caribbean. The reefs are stunning to look at. More importantly, they contain spectacular fishes, sponges, anemones, octopods, snails, marine reptiles, and other living things.

As corals grow, they create a complex structure that provides endless nooks and crannies for angelfish and other animals to live in.

The corals themselves build the homes for these incredible communities. Although they look like rocks, corals are living animals. As they grow, many corals make hard bony skeletons, which they leave behind when they die. Other corals build on these platforms. Over hundreds and thousands of years, huge coral reefs form. An explosion of

Coral reefs contain some of the highest levels of biodiversity on our planet. This candy-cane sea star makes its home among pale pink coral in the Red Sea.

species have evolved to live on coral reefs. So many different species live on reefs that scientists often call them the "rain forests of the seas."

This wealth of underwater life attracts armies of biologists wanting to learn more about the reefs. The scientists study how coral reef communities function, how reefs change over time, and how to protect the reefs while allowing humans to harvest fish and other reef resources. One of the most interesting things scientists study is how different reef species depend on one another to survive.

A Dependent World

The cleaner fish that Alexandra Grutter studies is just one of thousands of kinds of animals that have evolved close, dependent relationships with other living things. The nature of these relationships can vary, and scientists have several different names to describe them. Lexa, though, is especially interested in *mutualistic relationships,* or *mutualism.* In a mutualistic relationship, two different kinds of living things, or species, interact with each other in ways that help them both.

You can find mutualistic relationships almost everywhere you look. Bees, butterflies, and other insects, for instance, get nectar from flowers and pollinate the flowers at the same time. In tropical forests, certain kinds of trees produce food for ants and, in return, the ants defend the trees against leaf-eating insects. Almost nowhere, however, are mutualistic relationships more fascinating—and more important—than on coral reefs. Without mutualistic relationships, in fact, coral reefs might not even exist.

Surprisingly, scientists have only begun to unlock the mysteries of reef relationships in the past few years. The discoveries that Lexa has made about cleaner fish have startled the scientific community. So have the discoveries by other biologists about clownfish, giant

Mutualistic relationships thrive on coral reefs. Here a clownfish looks out from its resting place in a sea anemone. The anemone provides the clownfish with protection from predators. In return, the clownfish drives away certain fish that feed on anemones.

clams, and corals themselves. Together, this new information reveals surprising secrets about our underwater world.

CHAPTER 2

Swimming into Biology

IKE MANY OTHER BIOLOGISTS, Alexandra Grutter's interest in science began with simple childhood curiosity.

"My father's a fisherman," Lexa explains. "There are five of us and I'm the oldest, so I was always the helper. When we'd go out fishing for halibut in Alaska, I always liked to cut up the fish to see what was inside of them. Sometimes when I was supposed to be cleaning the fish, my dad would look over at me and say, 'Hey, what are you doing?' and have a good laugh.

"When I was about thirteen," Lexa continues, "we went to this beach near Puerto Vallarta, Mexico, and it was the first time I used a mask and snorkel. It was just amazing. I remember diving down, and you know how your ears hurt when you dive deep? I was having so much fun, I said to myself, 'Forget about the ears. I want to see *more.*'"

OPPOSITE: Since she was a child, Lexa has pursued a passionate curiosity about our underwater world. Here she uses a net to better examine a coral reef inhabitant.

These early experiences made a deep impression on Lexa. As soon as she graduated from high school, the first thing she did was move to Hawaii and take a scuba diving course. Her original plan was to go to college and dive just for fun. She got so hooked on diving, however, that she dropped out of college and became a full-time diving instructor and guide. It was in Hawaii that Lexa met her first cleaner fish.

Early Questions

As a diving guide, Lexa often took people on underwater tours of Hawaiian coral reefs. Over time, Lexa learned the best dive places and even got to know individual coral reef fish. She especially loved showing off the cleaner wrasses and their cleaning stations.

Cleaner fish live on most of the world's coral reefs. Often working in pairs, the cleaner fish set up cleaning stations next to a rock or piece of coral. They advertise these stations by flashing their blue, black, and white striped bodies. Soon, other coral reef fish—the "clients"—begin lining up to get cleaned.

One at a time, each client fish settles into a cleaning pose, spreading out its fins and opening its mouth and gills. Then, the cleaner

A cleaner wrasse approaches a potential client.

fish dart up and down the client's body. They pick off bloodsucking parasites from the client's skin and even swim inside the client's gills and mouth. After one client is cleaned, another takes its place. Watching these busy little cleaners, Lexa asked herself all kinds of questions: Why did the client fish want to be cleaned? Did cleaning really help the client fish? What benefits, if any, did the cleaner wrasses get out of the deal?

A fish sits and "poses" so that a cleaner fish can remove parasites from its skin, mouth, and gills.

Lexa didn't know if she'd ever learn the answers to these questions, but she soon grew tired of just looking at things. She wanted to *discover* more about them. She decided to quit her diving job and return to college to finish her undergraduate degree, first in Hawaii and then at the University of California at Santa Barbara. Afterward, she moved to Queensland, Australia, to begin work on her doctorate, or PhD, degree in marine biology.

As part of her doctorate degree, Lexa had to conduct an original field research project. She wasn't sure what it should be. One day, though, she was sitting around with a couple of other scientists, and one of them started talking about cleaner fish. "Hey, I remember those from Hawaii," Lexa told herself. After doing a bit of reading on cleaners and their clients, Lexa decided she'd try to answer some of the questions she'd had about these unusual little fish.

CHAPTER 3

Biological
Trail Blazing

HEN SHE BEGAN HER RESEARCH, Lexa discovered that there was still a lot of uncertainty about cleaner fish. People had been studying cleaner fish for years, but different scientific studies often came up with different, conflicting results. Given this confusion, Lexa decided to start her research fresh, from the beginning.

Her first goal was to figure out exactly what the cleaner fish were eating. Studies in Hawaii had indicated that they were eating mostly the mucus off the skins of the client fish, so Lexa began by focusing on that.

"I spent my first year looking at mucus," Lexa says. "I scraped it off of other fish and had this little vacuum collector, vacuuming mucus off things. But when I actually started looking at the guts of cleaner fish in Australia, I found that they were just so full of parasites, it made no

13

sense to look at mucus. 'Parasites!' I told myself. 'The cleaner fish are eating lots of parasites!'"

From then on, Lexa focused her attention on the cleaner fish's favorite food, a parasite called a gnathiid isopod (NAY-thid I-so-pod).

Lexa's early investigations quickly led her to look at parasites, such as the one on this triplefin fish.

Fresh Fish Studies

One thing that helped Lexa was the fresh approach she brought to her research. Earlier scientific studies on Australia's Great Barrier Reef, for example, had concluded that gnathiid isopods infected only a few kinds of coral reef fish. Lexa, however, conducted her own study and discovered the exact opposite. She dived underwater, captured fish with a hand net, and took a close look at them. She discovered that more than 70 percent of the fish species she caught were infected by gnathiid isopods. This helped confirm to her that the parasites must play a critical role in the life of the cleaner fish.

Next, Lexa wanted to learn just how many of the gnathiid isopods the cleaner fish were eating. To find out, she and her husband, Mark, dived down first thing in the morning and waited for the cleaner fish to come out of the holes where they spent their nights sleeping. As the cleaner fish woke up and got to work, Lexa and Mark started to count how many times the cleaner fish nipped at the client fish during the cleaning sessions. Then, every few minutes, Lexa cut open a couple of cleaner fish to see how many parasites they'd actually swallowed.

Lexa's results astonished her—and many other scientists. From her observations, she calculated that each cleaner fish ate about *twelve hundred* gnathiid isopods every day. However, a big question remained: Did getting their parasites removed really *help* the client fish?

To Be Cleaned or Not to Be Cleaned, That Is the Question...

Figuring out whether cleaner fish actually helped client fish promised to be a difficult job—one that Lexa was not looking forward to. Earlier scientists had spent years removing cleaner fish from reefs to see if their absence harmed the client fish. Unfortunately, the scientists came up empty-handed. Their studies didn't tell them whether cleaner fish made any difference to other fish, and Lexa thought it might take her even longer to tackle the problem—if she could do it at all.

However, one day Lexa caught a client fish and put it in a plastic bag full of water. A few minutes later, she looked in the bag and saw a little black thing swimming around. "I looked closer, and it was one of these gnathiid isopods," Lexa recalls. "I'd just caught the fish and already,

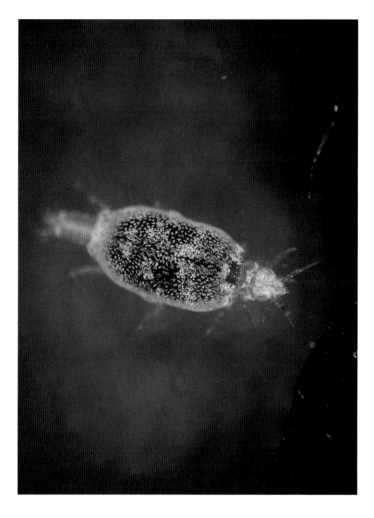

Gnathiid isopods are important parasites that infest many coral reef fishes.

this parasite had jumped off its host and was swimming around. That's when I realized that these parasites are really mobile."

Lexa soon discovered, in fact, that a gnathiid isopod can jump onto a fish, fill up with blood, and jump off again all in about an hour. This was something that other scientists had never realized before, and it gave Lexa an idea. Instead of looking at the effects of cleaner fish over very long time periods, maybe she should look at effects over very *short* periods.

A Day in the Life of Client Fish

In her first experiment, Lexa decided to count parasite numbers on individual client fish during the course of a single day. She put cages underwater on several different reefs, and into each cage she placed several parasite-free client fish. Some of the cages were on coral reefs with cleaner fish and others were on coral reefs where Lexa had removed the cleaner fish. Then she began counting the numbers of parasites on all of the caged fish during the next twenty-four hours.

Lexa began her experiment at sunset and found that during the night—when cleaner fish slept—all of the caged client fish became heavily infected with gnathiid isopods. It didn't matter what reef the cages were on: all of the client fish got a lot of parasites. As daylight began and the cleaner fish started cleaning, however, the situation began to change.

On the reefs without cleaner fish, parasite numbers remained high during the day. On the reefs with cleaner fish, the numbers of parasites on the client fish started to drop. By late afternoon, uncleaned client fish had *four and a half times* more parasites than the clients that were getting cleaned. This experiment didn't answer Lexa's original question of whether cleaner fish improved the health of client fish. But for the first time ever, a scientist had shown that cleaners can dramatically reduce the number of parasites on other fish species.

CHAPTER 4

Cleaning Up into the Future

N HER RESEARCH, Lexa has discovered that cleaner fish benefit from their relationship with client fish by getting to eat so many nutritious parasites. She's also proved that cleaner fish can reduce the numbers of parasites on client fish. However, she would still like to learn for certain whether removing parasites makes client fish healthier or not.

Lexa and other scientists have gathered indirect evidence that coral reef fish are healthier when they have fewer parasites. Several studies have shown that parasites can harm some kinds of fish by wounding them and reducing their rates of growth, reproduction, and survival. Parasites have also damaged and killed large numbers of salmon and other fish being raised in fish farms.

Still, no one has actually proved that removing parasites benefits

OPPOSITE: Lexa has tried many ideas to learn about cleaner fish. Here, she is training a cleaner to eat off of a small grid, or "plate."

Parasites such as sea lice infect farmed salmon and other commercial fish. Scientific research helps fish farmers keep their "crops" healthier.

the health of coral reef fish. To do that, Lexa has begun a series of studies that compares the condition of client fish with and without parasites. She hasn't completed her research yet, but in one study, large numbers of parasites were shown to reduce the number of red blood cells in client fish. With fewer red blood cells, client fish would be weakened and less able to fight disease. In another study, Lexa proved that reefs with cleaner fish support many more client fish than reefs where cleaner fish have been removed. She hopes that future studies will help her understand even more about the long-term benefits of cleaning—and why the cleaner-client relationship evolved in the first place.

Your Cheating Ways

Another research topic that fascinates Lexa is cheating. Instead of eating parasites, cleaner fish sometimes "cheat" by biting off pieces of the client fish's skin or scales—especially when there aren't enough parasites to go around. Client fish can also cheat by *eating* a cleaner fish! Lexa has wondered, "What keeps cleaner fish and client fish from cheating all the time?"

Lexa and fellow biologist Redouan Bshary have answered at least half of the question. Together, they closely observed hundreds of interactions between cleaner and client fish. They discovered that cleaner fish cheated a lot by biting off scales and skin instead of parasites. When they cheated too much, however, the client fish would "punish" them by chasing the cleaner fish. "It can be pretty funny," Lexa explains, "with the client chasing a cleaner round and round a coral head. What we found, though, is that fish that are 'punished' like this don't cheat as much in future interactions."

But what keeps a client fish from cheating by swallowing a cleaner fish? After all, a cleaner fish would make a tasty snack for a coral trout or other client. To find out, Lexa began by observing how cleaner fish behaved around hungry client fish compared to clients that were full. She noticed that cleaner fish spent a lot of time touching and rubbing against client fish. She calls this behavior "tactile dancing." Tactile dancing helps keep client fish from becoming aggressive and possibly eating the cleaners during a cleaning session.

"Bucket Science"

When most people think of science, they think of satellites, high-tech instruments, and elaborate computer systems. Some of a scientist's most useful equipment, however, is the simplest—such as the humble bucket.

"When I started my research," says Lexa, "I bought ten white buckets with very good lids from a butcher in Cairns. My work could not have succeeded without them! They have traveled with me to several research stations, and I've used them to hold hundreds and hundreds of fish during my experiments."

Lexa isn't the only scientist who loves buckets. "At the end of each trip," Lexa says, "I go around and count all my buckets and lids and have to do some serious hunting around for them. They always try to escape, and other researchers LOVE them and want to give them a holiday on their boats and in their labs."

Lexa's buckets like to wander away, but she always brings them home again.

What's especially interesting, however, is that the cleaners spend *more* time touching hungry client fish than those that aren't hungry. This indicates that cleaner fish can somehow recognize when client fish are hungry (although Lexa isn't sure how). It also shows that cleaners know that hungry clients are more dangerous than full clients—and that the cleaners must spend more time keeping those hungry clients calm.

Unfortunately, tactile dancing doesn't always work. Three times, Lexa saw client fish gulp down the cleaners that were trying to clean them. Overall, though, both clients and cleaner fish have evolved effective behaviors to keep cheating to a minimum and make sure everyone "plays fair" on the coral reef.

CHAPTER 5

Other Reef Relations

Coral Reef Clowns

As amazing as the cleaner-client relationship is, it is only one of many coral reef relationships that scientists have been studying. Another is the relationship between clownfish and the sea anemones they live with.

Twenty-seven species of clownfish live in tropical oceans. Most depend on a mutualistic relationship with certain kinds of sea anemones to survive. The clownfish gain protection from predators by hanging out among the sea anemones' poisonous tentacles. In return, the clownfish drive away butterflyfish and other fish that feed on the tentacles of the anemones.

One question biologists have asked is, "Why doesn't the clownfish get stung by the sea anemones?" Do the clownfish have some natural protection from the anemones' stingers, or do the clownfish somehow acquire protection? The answer, it turns out, is "both."

OPPOSITE: One of the most famous reef relationships is the one between clownfish and their deadly sea anemone hosts.

By exposing different clownfish species to different sea anemones, scientists have discovered that certain kinds of clownfish are born with *some* protection from their anemones. In other words, something about the clownfish makes their anemones less likely to sting them. All clownfish, however, can also acquire protection through a process called *acclimation*. During acclimation, a clownfish carefully works its way into an anemone's tentacles. As it does this, certain chemicals that belong to the anemone rub off on the mucus coating of the clownfish's skin. After acclimation, this mucus coating sends a chemical signal back to the anemone: "Don't shoot, it's me!"

One hitch is that acclimation only lasts a short time. Clownfish have to go through acclimation over and over, usually thousands of times,

While clownfish have protection from their sea anemones, other underwater inhabitants, such as these butterflyfish, do not.

during their lives. By doing so, they are able to live safely within the anemone's protective "arms."

Colossal Clams

Another remarkable reef relation-ship can be found inside the giant clams of Australia and Southeast Asia. Several dozen species of giant clams live in the region. The largest, *Tridacna gigas,* weighs up to five hundred pounds and has a shell three feet long. The clams don't reach these sizes alone. Inside of their tis-sues live thousands of single-celled organisms called *zooxanthellae* (ZOE-zan-THEL-ee). The zooxanthellae live close to the surface of the clam's tissue, where they can absorb sun-light shining down from above. Why is this important?

In the normal process of living, giant clams—like other animals—give off carbon dioxide and other waste products. Normally, these waste

Giant clams like this *Tridacna gigas* grow at remarkable rates thanks to the zooxanthellae that live inside them.

products are just swept away in the ocean. Zooxanthellae, however, cap-ture these waste products and turn them into food using sunlight and *photosynthesis.* This is a great deal both for the clam and the zooxanthellae. The zooxanthellae get nutrients (the clam's waste products) and a safe place to live inside the clam's tissues. In return, they manufacture food to help the clam live and grow.

One thing biologists have tried to figure out about this relationship is just *how much* of the clam's food the zooxanthellae provide. Giant clams don't obtain food solely from the zooxanthellae. Like other clams, they also filter food out of the water. This raises a natural question: Does a clam get most of its food by filter feeding, or from its zooxanthellae?

To find out, biologists compared the amount of food the clams get from their zooxanthellae to the amount they get from filter feeding. They discovered that filter feeding provides most of the food for younger clams. As the clams grow, however, the zooxanthellae provide more and more food. By the time *Tridacna gigas* weighs a few ounces, it gets about two-thirds of its food energy from the zooxanthellae.

How much food the zooxanthellae provide depends on the kind of clam. *Tridacna gigas,* for instance, gains twice as much food from its zooxanthellae as some other clam species. Not surprisingly, *Tridacna gigas* also grows much faster than most other kinds of clams.

Incomparable Corals

Clams are not the only animals that benefit from zooxanthellae. These photosynthetic "power plants" help feed various sponges, jellyfish, anemones, sea slugs, and—most important of all—corals.

Corals are closely related to jellyfish and sea anemones. Like their relatives, corals use tiny stinging tentacles to capture and eat small prey. Corals live in all oceans. They can be found in cold arctic waters and in waters deeper than the strongest sunlight can reach. However, the corals that grow into reefs live only in tropical, shallow waters that receive a lot of sunlight. Reef-building corals also have one other thing in common: they all have zooxanthellae living inside of them.

Many scientists believe that without zooxanthellae, corals would never be able to gather enough food energy to build reefs. Growing a hard, bony skeleton takes a lot of energy and, in a reef-building coral, most of this energy is provided by the zooxanthellae. Some kinds of corals do build a hard skeleton without zooxanthellae, but these corals never grow into reefs. Only corals with zooxanthellae have built the spectacular reefs we find today—including the

Corals, like their sea anemone relatives, use their stinging tentacles to capture and eat small prey.

Ideal conditions along Australia's east coast have produced the world's most spectacular reef complex, the Great Barrier Reef.

Great Barrier Reef, which consists of more than 3,000 separate reefs and stretches more than 1,200 miles along the east coast of Australia. Human beings benefit greatly from the productivity of reef-building corals. A huge number of people make their living from the fish and other animals that coral reefs provide. Coral reefs also protect shorelines from erosion and provide enjoyment for millions of scuba divers and other tourists. Because reefs are so important, biologists spend a lot of time studying them. They especially look at anything that might threaten these underwater treasures. One of these threats is *coral bleaching.*

Bleached to the Bone

Coral bleaching occurs when corals "kick out" their zooxanthellae. Zooxanthellae give corals their spectacular bright colors, and without them, corals look white or "bleached" like bones. Bleaching can be bad news for the corals. When bleaching happens, many corals die. In 1998, bleaching affected 16 percent of the world's coral reefs. On some of these reefs, all of the corals died—including some giant coral colonies up to seven hundred years old.

Many things can trigger bleaching, including pollution and heavy rains, but the most common culprit is unusually warm temperatures. The tropical waters where reefs occur

Coral bleaching often results in the deaths of living corals.

have different temperature ranges. When temperatures exceed the normal maximum average by only about two degrees Fahrenheit (one degree Celsius), bleaching begins. If cooler temperatures quickly return, many of the corals can recover and regain their zooxanthellae. But when warm temperatures last for more than a few days—as they did in 1998—corals begin to die.

Even though scientists understand what triggers coral bleaching, they have long been puzzled about *why* it occurs. Recently, however, scientists at the University of Queensland, Australia, think they've figured it out. These researchers discovered that when a coral gets too hot, its zooxanthellae stop photosynthesizing. Instead, incoming sunlight starts producing substances called "free radicals" inside the zooxanthellae. These free radicals are toxic to corals. To avoid being poisoned by them, the corals boot out their zooxanthellae. This strategy has probably saved corals countless times in the past. Nothing, however, seems to help corals survive extended heat waves like the one in 1998.

31

Human Relationships with the Reef

CORAL REEF RELATIONSHIPS didn't develop overnight. They've evolved over thousands—often millions—of years. By studying these relationships, biologists have made important discoveries about how coral reefs and their inhabitants function. Their research has given us new insights into these remarkable underwater communities.

Scientific research also has had direct benefits for humans. Dr. Grutter's work on cleaner fish has helped fish farmers understand the behavior of parasites—and may help them raise healthier, parasite-free fish. Clownfish studies have led to improved methods for raising these fish for the aquarium trade—and helped keep people from taking too many wild clownfish from coral reefs.

OPPOSITE: People depend on reefs not just for enjoyment, but for food and many other resources.

In the Solomon Islands, scientists have experimented with raising giant clams for more than a decade. They've helped local people figure out the best and fastest ways to raise the clams on nearby coral reefs. Villagers can then sell these clams to the aquarium trade or, when they grow larger, for food. Either way, this research assists villagers in earning money and supporting themselves.

Coral Crisis

Biological research is playing an even more important role in helping us protect coral reefs themselves. For the past fifty years, coral reefs have been under attack from many directions. They have been damaged by pollution. They have been smothered by soil washing into the ocean from farms and construction projects. People have blasted reefs with dynamite and poisoned them with cyanide to catch fish. Aquarium collectors have robbed reefs of many of their spectacular species including shellfish, sea anemones, fish, and corals. Approximately 10 percent of the world's coral reefs have been severely damaged or destroyed. More than half are threatened.

Hundreds of scientists are keeping track of coral reefs and how they are degraded. Two organizations, Reef Check and the Global Coral Reef Monitoring Network, also use thousands of divers and other volunteers to assess the condition of coral reefs all over the world. These programs provide up-to-date information that local, regional, and national governments can use to protect their coral reefs.

However, despite all of these efforts, one threat looms over the world's coral reefs: *global warming.*

The Big Burn

As the 1998 bleaching event showed, hot temperatures can be fatal to corals. The year 1998, however, was only one of many bleaching events on record. In the past twenty years alone, scientists have witnessed more than half a dozen major bleaching episodes throughout the world. Some of these events may be natural, but mounting evidence links coral bleaching to global warming.

Over the past century, Earth's average temperature has increased by about one degree Fahrenheit. This may not sound like much, but the rate at which the earth is heating up is getting faster and faster. The year 1998 was the hottest on record, but it probably won't be for long. Most of the 1990s—as well as the years 2001 through 2004—were unusually hot. Why is this happening? An overwhelming number of scientists believe that humans are to blame.

Since the start of the industrial age, people have been burning enormous amounts of coal, oil, and natural gas to produce energy.

This chart shows that Earth's temperatures have rapidly increased in recent decades—a potential catastrophe for coral reef communities.

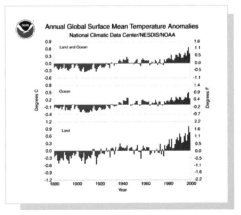

Automobiles alone burn more than thirty *billion* gallons of gasoline each year. When we burn these fossil fuels, we release millions of tons of the gas carbon dioxide into the atmosphere. Unfortunately, carbon dioxide and other "greenhouse gases" trap heat in our atmosphere and prevent it from escaping back into space. The result is that our planet is getting warmer and warmer.

As the amount of greenhouse gases keeps increasing, scientists believe that Earth's temperatures will continue to rise. Over the next century, temperatures are predicted to rise another three to seven degrees Fahrenheit. And as the air gets warmer, so will ocean waters. Bleaching events will become more frequent and more severe, and many coral reefs may disappear forever.

Scientists Sound the Alarm

Scientists are working hard to understand what's happening to coral reefs and to warn governments of the dire consequences of human activities. Governments have begun to take notice. In many parts of the world, nations have taken action to protect their coral reefs. By the year 2004, 122 nations had approved a treaty pledging to control and reduce the levels of greenhouse gases in the atmosphere. Instead of burning fossil fuels to produce energy, people worldwide are recognizing the importance of harnessing energy from the sun and wind. Conservation programs are also helping people reduce their consumption of electricity.

Unfortunately, the world's largest producer of greenhouse gases—the United States—has not done enough to help. Pressured by powerful oil and automobile companies, our government has refused to wean its

Wind power is one of many solutions that can reduce greenhouse gases and help protect our planet.

citizens from fossil fuels or to take meaningful steps to conserve energy. Many individual Americans also do not understand the need to reduce their energy consumption.

Armed with the information that scientists provide, however, we, as American citizens, can do our part. We can take steps to conserve energy. We can let our government know that we value coral reefs and are willing to do our part to save them. Turn to "What You Can Do to Help," following this chapter. Your efforts and concern *will* make a difference.

What You Can Do to Help

One of the easiest—and most important—things you can do to help protect coral reefs is to reduce the amount of energy you use. Most electricity and heat is produced by burning fossil fuels, an activity that many scientists believe increases Earth's temperatures and leads to coral bleaching. To reduce your energy consumption:

1) Always turn off lights and electrical appliances when you aren't using them. Urge your parents to replace regular lightbulbs with energy-saving compact fluorescent bulbs.

2) Walk, ride a bike, or carpool whenever you can.

3) Buy products that use less packaging. Making extra boxes, wrappers, and containers uses a lot of energy that could be saved.

4) Take shorter showers.

5) Recycle bottles, cans, and newspapers.

6) Encourage your friends and family to take these actions, too.

In addition, write to the president, your congressman, senators, and other elected representatives. Encourage them to commit to reducing our nation's production of greenhouse gases. Ask them to pass laws that require higher mileage standards for automobiles. Tell them you support more spending for mass transit and for developing alternative energy such as solar and wind power. The president's address is:

The White House
1600 Pennsylvania Ave. NW
Washington, DC 20500

You can send him an e-mail at: president@whitehouse.gov

To find the addresses of your own members of Congress, log on to the *Contacting the Congress* Web site at: http://www.visi.com/juan/congress/

How U.S. Reefs Are Doing

The United States is home to several large coral reef systems. Along the mainland, reefs are found only in the Florida Keys. But offshore, reefs occur in Hawaii, Puerto Rico, the Virgin Islands, and the Gulf of Mexico, as well as Guam and other U.S.-owned Pacific islands. Unfortunately, U.S. reefs have suffered many of the same injuries as other reefs around the world. Some reefs in Hawaii and other remote locations remain in good condition. Others, such as those in the Florida Keys, have been extensively damaged. Causes of reef damage include overfishing, crushing from anchors and ships, runoff of sewage and sediments from land, coral disease, and bleaching. The U.S. government has made some effort to protect remaining reefs. Until we get serious about reversing global warming, however, reefs will probably continue to deteriorate.

Glossary

ACCLIMATION a process of adjusting—in the case of the clownfish, by slowly obtaining the chemicals that prevent an anemone from stinging it

CORAL BLEACHING the whitening of coral reefs that results when corals eject the zooxanthellae living inside of them

EROSION the "wearing away" of coastlines and other geographic features by wind, waves, and other elements

EVOLUTION (EVOLVE, EVOLVED) the process by which species change over time via mutations that happen in their DNA; evolution is also what creates new species from older ones

GLOBAL WARMING the rise in temperatures caused by an increase of gases that trap the heat in Earth's atmosphere

GREENHOUSE GASES carbon dioxide and other gases that trap heat inside of Earth's atmosphere, leading to global warming

ISOPOD a large group of invertebrates with hard shells and, usually, flattened bodies; they are closely related to crabs, shrimp, and barnacles

MUTUALISM, MUTUALISTIC RELATIONSHIP a relationship in which two different species live or behave in a way that benefits both of them; sometimes mutualism is called "symbiosis"

PARASITE an organism that obtains food or nutrition from another organism, or host, in a manner that harms the host

PHOTOSYNTHESIS the process by which certain organisms use the sun's energy to make food

ZOOXANTHELLAE a group of tiny, single-celled organisms that live inside the bodies of other animals in a mutualistic relationship

To Learn More

Books

Cerullo, Mary. *Coral Reef: A City That Never Sleeps.* New York: Cobblehill Books, 1996.

Collard, Sneed B. *Lizard Island: Science and Scientists on Australia's Great Barrier Reef.* Danbury, CT: Franklin Watts, 2000.

Pringle, Laurence. *Coral Reefs: Earth's Undersea Treasures.* New York: Simon and Schuster, 1995.

Pringle, Laurence. *Global Warming: The Threat of Earth's Changing Climate.* New York: Sea Star Books, 2001.

Internet Sites

Dozens of outstanding Web sites about coral reefs and global warming can be found on the Internet. Here are a few:

http://www.lexagrutter.com/
> *The Web site of Dr. Alexandra Grutter, this site presents her latest discoveries and provides links to other Web sites about cleaner fish, mutualism, and marine science.*

www.aims.gov.au/index-ie.html
> *This site of the Australian Institute of Marine Science presents a variety of information on Australian and worldwide reefs, including scientific research, status updates, and conservation efforts. You can also find a copy of the book* Status of Coral Reefs of the World 2000 *here.*

www.coralreefalliance.org
> *The Coral Reef Alliance is dedicated to protecting coral reefs around the world. This site contains conservation information and links to other great reef sites.*

www.epa.gov/owow/oceans/coral/
> *An Environmental Protection Agency site, describing U.S. policies and activities aimed at protecting coral reefs.*

www.coral.aoml.noaa.gov/gcrmn/
> *Site of the Global Coral Reef Monitoring Network, providing the latest information on the status of coral reefs all over the world.*

www.wri.org
> *World Resources Institute site focusing on a variety of environmental problems and solutions, including global warming, loss of biodiversity, and overpopulation.*

Index

About the Author

SNEED B. COLLARD III has written more than fifty books for young people. They include the popular picture books *Animal Dads, Leaving Home,* and *Animals Asleep* as well as in-depth science books such as *Monteverde: Science and Scientists in a Costa Rican Cloud Forest.* His books *The Forest in the Clouds* and *Beaks!* were both named Teacher's Choices by the International Reading Association, and many of his other titles have received similar recognition. Before beginning his writing career, Sneed graduated with honors in biology from the University of California at Berkeley. To research and photograph the SCIENCE ADVENTURES series, he visited Costa Rica's cloud forest, Australia's Great Barrier Reef, Zoo Atlanta, and the deep-sea floor. Sneed lives in Missoula, Montana, where he enjoys observing nature during long walks with his border collie, Mattie. His Web site is: www.sneedbcollardiii.com